BYRON KATIE

❦ *on* ❧

Parents and Children

Edited by Stephen Mitchell

the work of
byron katie
WWW.THEWORK.COM

BYRON KATIE INTERNATIONAL, INC. • LOS ANGELES

Published in the United States by:
Byron Katie International, Inc.
578 Washington Blvd. Box 821
Marina del Rey, CA 90292
1-800-98KATIE (52843)
www.thework.com

ISBN 1-890246-79-4

Printed in the United States of America.
Design & Layout by Balsam Design
Art Director: Richard Balsam
Production Specialist: Emily Eoff
Cover Photography: Brie Childers

To Michele Penner
and to Ellen Mack,
with love and gratitude

The Work of Byron Katie:
The Four Questions and Turnaround

1. Is it true?
2. Can you absolutely know that it's true?
3. How do you react when you believe that thought?
4. Who would you be without the thought?
   and

Turn it around.

Here's what I've told my children: "You have the perfect mother. I'm responsible for all your problems, and you're responsible for the solutions."

Our parents, our children, our spouses, and our friends will continue to press every button we have, until we realize what it is that we don't want to know about ourselves, yet. They will point us to our freedom every time.

"Mothers are supposed to love their daughters"—is that true? It's an old, old myth. It's as old as the dinosaurs. The way you can know it isn't true is that every time you believe it, you hurt. That's because it is not your nature. When you believe it, you're in a lie. You know how a mother bird pushes her chicks out of the nest? "You're out of here," she says. That's love. She doesn't say, "I love you: stay." She says, "I love you: fly." We can give you at least what a bird will give! So how do you react every time you believe the lie that your mother should love you? Separation. Who would you be in your mother's presence if you didn't have the ability to think the thought that she should love you? At peace, a listener, just loving her the way she is. "Your mother should love you"—turn it around. You should love you. It's your job to love you. "I don't love myself, so you do it"—what's wrong with this picture? So you do it, and the way you do it is to stay present, and every time you do that, you fall in love with yourself, because you are the truth. And when your mother says something, all you hear is the sound of God, because God is everything, there isn't anything else. Until you can see your mother as God, your Work isn't done.

Parents can't be the problem. The Work is about 100 percent responsibility. This is very good news. It means there are no parents to change. There is only investigation.

You can't make people happy. My daughter wanted a car. It was not an easy time in her life. She was so beautiful and dear and yet filled with self-hatred, guilt, and shame. I felt this was the perfect opportunity to make her happy, and I bought her a car. I thought the car was fabulous. I pictured her in it, and felt an all-consuming pleasure. I gave it to her, and my heart was pounding with excitement from beginning to end. It was the gift of a lifetime, and I was giving her the key to happiness. Her friends did not own cars. She was just turning sixteen. I presented the car to her, and I could see right away that something was wrong. She wasn't happy. It wasn't the car she wanted. (It was the kind of car that her friends would tease her about, and I had no way of knowing that.) At the time I was deluded enough to believe that she should be grateful, that she should love it, and that she was being difficult on purpose. I came to see that she was just like me. If anyone is going to make me happy, it has to be me, and she will find her own happiness or not. I came to see that it was all about me.

We're all five-year-olds. We don't know how to do this thing called life. We're just learning how.

If you think you are supposed to love your children, you're in big trouble. It just sets you up for shame and guilt. You're not supposed to love your children until you do. How do you react when you believe the thought that you're supposed to love them? Fear, depression, resentment, self-hatred. Maybe you feel like a freak, like there's something terribly wrong with you, some essential ingredient missing. Who would you be without the belief that you're supposed to love your children right now? You'd be free to love them or not, and to be a very good parent, whatever you're feeling right now. Then you can find your love, you can hear them now, you can be with them now, you don't have to do anything or be anything. Inquiry sets us free of trying to be anything we're not.

My children should be happy so that I can be happy? That doesn't sound like love to me. I think I'll just skip them and be happy from here! It's a lot saner. It's called unconditional love.

God is another name for reality, and I am a lover of what is. If I lose my grandchild or my daughter, I lose what wasn't mine in the first place. It's a good thing. Either that, or God is a sadist, and that's not my experience. I don't order God around. I don't presume to know whether life or death is better for me or for anyone I love. How can I know that? All I know is that God is everything and God is good. That's my story, and I'm sticking to it.

What's true for me is that in no way do I want my children's approval. That would assume I don't have it anyway. To want their approval would be to rape their minds. It would be to direct their minds to me when their minds are directed to where they're supposed to be.

"Parents are not supposed to attach to children"—what's the reality of it? Do they? So is it true that parents are not supposed to attach? It's not true. I call it a flat-out lie. I call it that so it can be heard. How do you treat your mother or father when you believe that they're not supposed to attach to you? You pull away and feel superior. Who would you be without this story? Close your eyes. Look at your mother attaching to you. Look at her face, look at her body. Look at her without your story. What do you see? A beautiful human being, someone you love with all your heart. And nothing has happened except that you're seeing what

is. When you attach to a story, you lose the
awareness of that love.

Do children understand The Work?
Absolutely. There are only concepts. There
are no adults, there are no children. Concepts
are ageless. Here's what children say: "My
father should understand me." "My friends
should listen to me." "Mommy shouldn't fight
with Daddy." "I want you to love me." By the
time they're four or five, children believe
exactly the same stressful thoughts that

adults believe. There are no new concepts.
Children are just as confused as adults.

My children tell me what they want all the
time. And I just hear them. What does that
have to do with me? They're just expressing
their wants. Those wants are their property.
I have mine, they have theirs. When they
give me their wants, can I just listen, without
thinking it's about me? That's what we all
want from our parents. Just someone to
understand, to hear us. We may think we want
other things, but that's what we really want.

My job is to stay out of my children's business and to love them instead.

If your husband doesn't take care of the kids, does that mean that you don't get to do your own thing? Really? What stops you? How can anyone stop you from doing your own thing? If you want to do something without the kids, you can leave them. You can just leave them, and go off and do what you want to do. But you don't. You stay with them because you want something more than to leave. Your husband has nothing to do with it. You can leave anytime. Isn't that fine to know? When you believe that you can't do what you want because of him, you're lost in a dream. It's the dream that you're stuck that makes you stuck. No mother ever had to stay with her children. We just like to tell the story of how we have to, and in that story we end up beating them, hating our husbands, divorcing, going nuts. Who would you be without this lie?

Babies are not born into this world of illusion until they attach. When you're clear, it's wonderful fun to observe it. I love being with my grandbabies. I love hearing all my lies! "That's a tree." "That's a sky." "I love you." "You're Grandma's precious." "You're the sweetest thing I've ever seen!" All these lies, and I'm having a wonderful time. If it doesn't work for them, they can question their stressful thoughts. I am joy. I'm not going to censor any of it.

Your husband shouldn't go check his e-mail and be gone for hours? Hopeless! Children and family cannot compete with e-mail! That's it. How do you treat him when you attach to this story that he should prefer you and the family to the internet! Are you the teacher of shame and guilt? How does that feel inside you? Who would you be without the story that he should prefer you to the internet?

People often ask me if I had a religion before 1986, and I say yes—it was "My children should pick up their socks." This was my religion, and I was totally devoted to it, even though it never worked. Then one day, after The Work was alive in me, I realized that it simply wasn't true. The reality was that day after day, they left their socks on the floor, after all my years of preaching and nagging and punishing them. I saw that *I* was the one who should pick up the socks if I wanted them picked up. My children were perfectly happy with their socks on the floor. Who had the problem? It was me. It was my thoughts about the socks on the floor that had made my life difficult, not the socks themselves. And who had the solution? Again, me. I realized that I could be right, or I could be free. It took just a few moments for me to pick up the socks, without any thought of my children. And an amazing thing began to happen. I realized that I loved picking up their socks. It was for me, not for them. It stopped being a chore in that moment, and it became a pleasure to pick them up and see the uncluttered floor. Eventually, they noticed my pleasure and began to pick up their socks on their own, without my having to say anything.

Like-minded? My whole family is like-minded. They lie on the floor, they walk, they sit, they tell stories. That's about it. None of the stories is true. They just have a wonderful time. It's a great movie. They tell the story of how I love them or I don't. It's all just a story.

Here's how a child listens. You tell a child something. The child puts his own interpretation on what you said. That's what the child hears. No one has ever heard you.

If one of my children were to say, "I hate you," I would say, "Let me be with that a minute. I understand—look how I treated you all those years. I understand that. What can I do? What do you suggest?" If he or she said, "Screw you with your spiritual talk! I never want to see you again," I wouldn't say lovingly, "I understand." I'm a listener. I go inside and understand. I don't have to share that understanding with them at that point. If I said "I love you," it would like taking a knife and sticking it into their heart.

You are the mother you've been waiting for. When you focus on your mother, you become motherless.

You enter this Work, and your children, your spouse, your parents will give you everything you need to get free. The whole world will. It's all a reflection of you. It's perfect. There are no accidents.

You want your mother not to get the cancer back again. What for? So she can be a mother to you? Is she supposed to stay alive for your sake? She can't even live or die, except for you. Interesting, isn't it? Do you even care if she lives except to make you happy? You think she likes living—what does that have to do with you? Nothing. Interesting, isn't it? You might go home and say, "Mom, I just discovered I want you to stay alive so that I can be happy. And by the way, I love you."

I was a child at forty-three. I came to see that I didn't know anything. I didn't know how to live. I had this Work, and I noticed I was being lived. I was like a child, a toddler. It was so much fun! Especially when we stay in The Work and come to see we don't have to know anything. The whole world will give us everything we need.

Your child says you're stupid. He could be right! I can go there. Who knows how to raise a child? All of us are pretty stupid about that. All he said is that you're stupid—why would you argue with that? Who would be stupid enough to argue with someone they love, if they had another way? You could just say, "Sweetheart, what do you suggest? I do feel stupid. I love you, and I don't know how to do it." That's the truth of it. We'd all do that if we knew how. And that's the power of this Work—living the turnarounds. Living the answers that we find here. You could go home and say to your son, "You've been telling me I'm stupid, and I found it. I was the last to

know. And what I'm stupid about is that I
don't know how to love you. I need your help.
I want to hear you."

Can I do what I wanted my parents to do?
Can I give myself what I wanted my parents
to give me? This is a life's work. Some of us
don't know how. And we expect our parents to
have known how. Everything you want them
to give you, turn it around, and give it to
yourself. Life is good. I have myself now. And
then everything I want, I give you too. And I
feel such joy. I come to see that that is the gift

I give myself. But until I gave it to myself, I couldn't give it to you. And to give it to you is to give it to my very own self.

❧

When my daughter, Roxann, did her first workshop with me, it was in 1993 with a large group of therapists present. She was working on "the mother from hell"—which was how she had experienced me as she was growing up—and she couldn't even bear to look at me, she couldn't bear to hear the sound of my voice. I was the root of her problem, she thought, and I was also her salvation, she had

to ask the monster for help, which made her
furious. And at a certain moment she became
very passionate and got right in my face and
said I should have mothered her. I said, "I will
never be the mother you want. I can't be. It's
not my job. Mother yourself!" And she shared
with me later that that was the greatest gift I
ever gave her. It turned out to be her freedom.
I know the privilege of mothering myself. It's
hopeless to see it as anyone else's job.

The bottom line is that your mother does
love you—there's nothing she can do about

that. Just don't expect her to be aware of that.
Your mother loves you so much that she would
withhold love so you can get this thing, this
self-love thing. You can't love her until you
do that. If I hate me, I hate my mother. If I
love me, I love my mother. It's that simple.

Eventually the stressful concepts come
and we're lit, we walk down the street like a
thousand-watt light bulb. A concept like "I
need my mother to love me" comes in and we
just laugh. We laugh because we're awake to
that concept, and the next, and the next.

You can't disappoint another human being.
And another human being can't disappoint
you. You tell the story of how someone is not
giving you what you want, and you disappoint
you. If you want something from your mother
and she says no, that's it. You need to give
it to yourself. This is good news, because it
allows you to get what you want. If you don't
have her to help you, you have you to help you.
If she says no, it leaves you.

Self-inquiry is the mind giving itself its own
story back. When we were children, the world

said, "The sky is blue." So we said, "The sky is blue." We didn't stop to go inside and ask ourselves. We didn't know how. So we begin now. But with a little child, the mother says, "The sky is blue." And a wise child would go inside. "Can I really know that that's true? No. I can see it's my mother's religion, it just doesn't happen to be mine. And what she's got is equally as valuable as what I've got. So we love. She says it's blue, I say I understand. And I don't bother to tell her that it's not my experience. And if she asks me, I'm going to say, 'You know, mother, it's not my experience, and I love that you see that the sky is blue. We're compatible.'"

You know why we don't want our families to die? They hold the story of our past. Without them, we have to get a stranger, pretend to make friends with him, tell him our story of the past, so that when we're standing there with someone else to impress, we can turn and say, "Isn't that right!" To get him to hold up what is not true for us. There goes your history! It leaves you here now.

I can be with my son and say, "Sweetheart, I see your pain. What can I do? I love you. If you can see a role for me to take here, to help

you in any way, I'll do it. I love you. I'm here."
And then you can hold him. But fear can't
end fear. Your pain cannot end his pain. And
if he says, "Oh, no, Mom, you can't help me.
Go away," then I hear him. Good. How clear
is that! So I go away. That leaves him to heal
himself. He's with the master, the teacher. I
don't teach him that I am the source of his
happiness. That would be crazy. What would
happen when I die? He'd lose the source of
his happiness. To give him back himself—
that's love.

It's painful to think that we know what's best
for our children. It's hopeless.

"Your mother should love you"—is that true?
This is the death of a dream. Can you see one
good reason to keep the story that *anyone*
should love you, ever? Have you ever tried
to love your perceived enemy? It's hopeless.
Who would you be without this story that
your mother should love you? You'd be
you, without all that efforting. Without the
mask, the façade. It feels like freedom to me.
Wanting your mother to love you is like being

in a strait jacket: "Love me! Love me!" It's like being a dog on the floor just crawling and begging, with your tongue hanging out: "Love me! Love me! I'll be good! I'll be good!" Make a list of everything you want her to do for you, then do it for yourself, and do it now. This is the real thing. You want it from her? Turn it around and live it yourself.

Can you know that your daughters won't be better off without their mother? This is a big one: "Children are much better off with their mothers"—is that true? This is the world's favorite religion, and can you absolutely know that it's true? I'm not saying that they aren't better off with her. This Work is an investigation, it's not about anything else, it's for you to go inside and find out. I'm so greedy, I want it all, so I love, and I have it all. And any obstacle can only be a story. I investigate, and I am the experience of the awareness of love now—pure greed. When mothers remain with their children, how do I know that it's for their children's highest good? There they are! When mothers don't remain with their children, how do I know that *that's* for their children's highest good? They aren't there! Either that, or God is a

sadist and the universe is chaos, and that is
not my experience. That was my experience
for forty-three years, but with this Work, I
can only see perfect order. There is nothing
terrible. Investigation is the way through
to reality.

When you stay out of your family's business,
they notice that you have your stuff together
and that you're happy, so they start to follow.
You have taught them everything they know,
and now they begin to learn again. And that's
what happened with my children, they just

don't see a lot of problems anymore, because in the presence of someone who doesn't have a problem, they can't hold on to one.

Mothers are always right—they love that! Have you ever changed your mother's mind? It's not as though we have a choice. Your mother gets to be right all your life, but if your mind is open, you get to be free.

If your truth now is kind, it will run deep and fast within the family and will replace manipulation with a better way. As you continue to find your own way in inquiry, sooner or later your family will come to see as you yourself do. There's no other choice. Your family is a projected image of your thinking. It's your story; nothing else is possible. Until you love your family without conditions, self-love is not a possibility, and therefore your Work is not done.

How do you treat your children when you want
them to love you and they don't? Can you see
any reason that is not stressful to want them
to love you, or to want anyone on this planet
to love you? If I have the thought I want my
children to love me, it isn't love. I want them
to love whoever they love—I may as well,
because that's what they do. I can't redirect it.
I'm not a fool anymore. And people call that
love, but I am just a lover of what is. And I
know the joy of loving, so I don't care how they
direct it. Who would you be without the story
"I want them to love me"? To love your children
is to love yourself. To love yourself is to love

your children. The story "I want them to love me" just keeps you from the awareness of love.

When my children say, "Mom, what should I do?" I tell them the truth: "I don't know, honey. I can't know what's best for you. Here's what I did in a similar situation, and it worked for me. And you can always know that I'm here to listen and that I'm always going to love you, whatever decision you make. You'll know what to do. And also, sweetheart, you can't do it wrong. I promise you that." I finally

learned to tell my children the truth, and they
trust that, and I trust it.

Your family will see you as they see you, and
that will leave you to work on them all. How
do you see *yourself*? That's the important
question. How do you see *them*? If I think that
they need The Work, then I need The Work.
Peace doesn't require two people; it requires
only one. It has to be you. The problem begins
and ends there.

"Children should love their parents"—is it true? It didn't work for me, so I gave that concept up. If it hurts, I give it up. I live internally. I always have. It's just that now I notice. My children should love me? Not ever. I should love my children: let me live the theory, especially when they don't call. If I want to hear my daughter, I call her, I hear her voice. I do it for my sake, she has nothing to do with it. I call, I get my daughter-fix, I am nourished, I hang up. I love when I do that.

Whose business are my children? Their business! When we're mentally out of our children's business, we have a shot at happiness, and so do they, because finally there's an example in the house.

How can you have rules and still stay out of your children's business? Drop the rules and find out! You'll find that your children, on their own, will live every rule you've ever taught them, and some of them you may not like. They are a perfect reflection of you. They turned out to be you.

Ultimately you don't have any control over your children. You don't have any control over anything. When you think you do, and you see that you don't, the effect is depression.

Is it true that your children should be grateful that you were such a good parent? How do you treat them when they don't remember what a loving parent you have been? What do you say to them when they forget that you love them so unconditionally? How do you treat them when you want them to remember and be grateful, and they want nothing to do with it? Offended? Hurt? Are you beginning to understand why they're not real crazy about you sometimes? This is our religion: "My children should be grateful." Turn it around: *I* should be grateful that I was such a good parent. And be with that. It doesn't matter what the reason was, you were there when they were sick, you were there when they were well, you got them to school, you went to their performances, you read to them, you gave them birthday parties. It's not their job to be grateful, or even to remember. If you want a past, you keep it!

Who would you be in the presence of your child if you didn't believe the thought that you shouldn't have hit her in the past? You think guilt and shame are going to prevent you from hitting her again, but it's the opposite. You use that weapon to keep you from violence, and it is internal violence. It is internal violence to call yourself "bad" and "wrong." If you don't believe the thought that you shouldn't have hit her, you aren't living an internal violence. How do you know you should have hit her? You did. How did it feel: not okay? That's how you violated yourself. When you hit her, you are hitting yourself.

She really is God in human form here to
teach you that.

If you want to alienate your friends and
family, go around saying, "Is it true?" or "Turn
it around" if they're not asking you for help.
You may need to do that for a while, in order
to hear it for yourself. It's uncomfortable to
believe that you know more than your friends
and to represent yourself as their teacher.
Their irritation will lead you deeper into
inquiry or deeper into your suffering.

When you stay present with your children, that's where abundance is. And when you stay out of their business, that is where everything you deserve in life is, it's right there. When you are in presence, there's no story there, and you are abundance, everything you ever wanted is there in that moment, and you come to trust it. And you come to trust that space so often that you just eventually hang out as that, because there is nothing that can move you out of it, not even a perceived child or a perceived anything.

Why would I impose my will on my children when I can't possibly know what's best for them? If what they do brings them happiness, that's what I want; and if it brings them unhappiness, it's for me to see and celebrate the way of it, and to share with them, through my eyes, what they may have missed. If they don't see the good in the results, then they have missed something important, because the way of it is never unkind. I simply see what they haven't seen yet. They can see through my eyes that nothing bad is possible. Or not.

If your daughter killed herself, whose business is that? When you think you know what's best for her, it's not love. How can you know what's best for her? How can you know that life would be better for her than death? You would deprive her of her whole path. Who do you think you are? There's no respect there. If my daughter is going to take her life, and I know about it, I'm going to speak to her and offer myself in whatever way she thinks would be useful. And if she has killed herself, I'm not going to think, "Sweetheart, you should have stayed here for my sake. I know you were suffering abominably, but you really should have stayed here and suffered

so that I wouldn't feel terrible." Is that love?
And do you really want her to live in the
torture chamber of her own mind? When our
suffering gets too intense, we can inquire,
and if we don't have inquiry, some of us just
knock out our painful thoughts with a gun
or pills or whatever it takes, but we have to
shut this system down. And it's hell to open
your eyes in the morning when you have this
painful thought system going. Unconditional
love means that your children don't need
your permission to live or die. How do you
react when you believe the thought that she
shouldn't have taken her own life? You get to
experience hell. And who would you be if you

didn't believe the concept that she shouldn't have taken her own life? Who would you be without the story? You can't have your daughter as long as you have a concept of her. When you get rid of the concept, you meet your daughter for the first time. That's the way this works.

The advice you've been giving your family and friends turns out to be advice for you to live, not us. You become the wise teacher as you become a student of yourself. It stops mattering if anyone else hears you, because *you're* listening. You are the wisdom you offer us, breathing and walking and effortlessly moving on, as you make your business deal, buy your groceries, or do the dishes.

Self-realization is the sweetest thing. It shows us how we are fully responsible for ourselves, and that is where we find our freedom. Rather than being other-realized, you can be self-realized. Instead of looking to us for your fulfillment, you can find it in yourself.

If your happiness depends on your children being happy, that makes them your hostages. So stay out of their business, stop using them for your happiness, and be your own happiness. And that way you are the teacher for your children: someone who knows how to live a happy life.

"My parents are responsible for my belief systems and my problems"—is it true? No, I'm the one who's responsible. Knowing this gives us what we always wanted: absolute control. And with this technology of going inside, it's the end of suffering, if we want to be free.

When my daughter, Roxann, was sixteen, she drank very heavily and also did drugs. This had begun to happen before I woke up with the questions in 1986, but I was so depressed then that I was totally unaware of it. After inquiry was alive in me, though, I began to notice her actions as well as my thoughts about them. She used to drive off every night in her new red Camaro. If I asked where she was going, she would give me a furious look and slam the door on her way out. It was a look I understood well. I'd taught her to see me that way. I myself had worn that look on my face for many years. Through inquiry, I learned to become very quiet around her, around everyone. I learned how to be a listener. I would often sit and wait up for her far past midnight, for the pure privilege of seeing her—just for that privilege. I knew she was drinking, and I knew I couldn't do a thing about it. The thoughts that would appear in my mind were thoughts like these: "She's probably drunk and driving, and she'll be killed in a crash, and I'll never see her again. I'm her mother, I bought her the car,

I'm responsible. I should take her car from her (but it wasn't mine to take; I'd given it to her; it was hers); she'll drive while she's drunk, and she'll kill someone, she'll crash into another car or drive into a lamppost and kill herself and her passengers." As the thoughts appeared, each one would be met with wordless, thoughtless inquiry. And inquiry instantly brought me back to reality. Here is what was true: woman sitting in chair waiting for her beloved daughter. One evening, after being gone for a three-day weekend, Roxann came through the door with a look of great misery on her face and, it seemed to me, without any

defenses. She saw me sitting there, and she
just fell into my arms and said, "Mom, I can't
do this anymore. Please help me. Whatever
this thing is that you're giving to all these
people who come to our house, I want it." So
we did The Work, and she joined Alcoholics
Anonymous. That was the last time she did
alcohol or drugs. The Work can complement
any recovery program. Whenever she had a
problem after that, she didn't need to drink
or drug, and she didn't need me. She just
wrote the problem down, asked four questions,
and turned it around. When there's peace
here, there's peace there. To have a way to see

beyond the illusion of suffering is the greatest gift. I love that all my children have taken advantage of it.

Your family is an echo of your own past beliefs.

How do you react when you believe that someone you love is suffering? Whether she's suffering or not is her business, but how do you react when you believe the thought? You suffer, and then you have to leave the room, you have to leave the person you love. That's how you react when you believe that she's suffering. That thought keeps you out of the room you want to be in. So close your eyes, picture yourself in the room with your mother, without the belief that she's suffering, and without the belief that she's not supposed to. Is it fine to be in the room with her now? Of course it is. I adore my children, and I adore my grandchildren, and their suffering is their business. I let them have their suffering. They can live, they can die, and I love them, that's what I know. I love them enough to stay out of their business and be present. And I am

not being present on purpose, I just don't
have a reason to leave the room when they are
suffering, and in the presence of peace and
love, it can't hold.

"Parents are not supposed to judge you"—is
that true? And aren't you making a judgment
that your parents aren't supposed to judge?
Well, they're just doing what you do. If you
want them to stop, *you* try it. How do you
treat your parents when they judge you, and
you're attached to the belief that they're not
supposed to? That's our job, we judge. We've

been guided to stop judging for generations, and it's still what we do. Have you noticed that it's hopeless: no matter how you isolate from them, move away, no matter what external or internal tantrum you throw, they still judge you? That's what they do. A dog barks, a cat meows, and parents judge.

Parents can only be wise when they stop teaching.

Your parents don't have to be alive for you to do this Work on them. No one has to be alive for you to do this Work on them. They live in your mind. That's where you heal yourself. Those of you whose family are gone, it's perfect. And those of you who still have your family living, it's perfect. No mistake.

This is a very sweet way to communicate at home. Just ask your child to read her or his Worksheet to you. There is no right or wrong here, this is communication. And after every statement, just say "Thank you,"

nothing more. Love is a listener. This is about receiving. There's nothing more powerful than just to receive your daughter or son now. That is the giving, there is nothing more precious. On every one of the statements, did you go there? How many times did you want to defend when she read the Worksheet? What does her opinion have to do with you? This is the end of war, inside her, and therefore inside you.

Your parents are your projection—nothing more.

If you took your Worksheet to your mother or father and asked them just to be still all the way through and say "Thank you" after each statement, or if you just gave them each of the turnarounds to yourself, you would join them completely, because you can't say anything about yourself that they don't already know. On some level, they already know your greatest, darkest secret. It's no surprise.

It's not okay for me to yell at my son. I noticed that. It has nothing to do with the world's morality. So if I were ever angry at him, I would judge him, write it down, ask four questions, and turn it around, and notice that he is not my problem, I am my problem. My children really love it that I have this Work!

When your mind becomes clear, everything else follows. You step into the living of it, and then your job, your money, your children, and everything else follows. You get clear, and everything is cause and effect: I do this, I get that. That's the way of it.

Until I can understand myself, I can't even hear my parents. They are just my story. People who do this Work come to know their parents for the first time, even though their parents have been dead for thirty years.

Here's a meditation on a disapproving parent; you're welcome to do it if you think it would serve you. Close your eyes. Now look at your father, for example, with that disapproving look on his face. Now look at yourself on your favorite chair. Now reduce him to a child, a little boy. Now open your arms and invite him onto your lap. Invite the little guy onto your lap. Did he come? Now hold him, smell his little head, and his hair, just experience him there. Now tell him what you would like to tell him. Tell him you love him, if that's true. After you do this, you may have the most touching realizations. You may see that you care about your father the way you wanted him to care about you. It's the old turnaround trick. "I want him to love me": I want me to love him. We investigate the story, and the illusion is blown. And it brings up the next, so we can meet that one with understanding. And all the illusions start falling like dominoes.

I don't have relationships with my children anymore. I have intimacy instead.

৶

If I have the thought "I want my mother to love me," I'm insane. I turned it around: "I want me to love my mother." Let me live what I thought should be so easy for her. She should just drop her life and love me, I have no interest in her life, or what she wants, she should love me, I am clear, that's it. This isn't love. Can I just love without expecting anything in return? Can I live my own philosophy? And when I am in her presence,

I am a very humble woman, because I really try to live it. But if I expect her to, I'm in big trouble. And if I am not mentally directing who she loves, it feels like self-love, because I see how I treat her when I want her love, and it's not a pretty sight. So I become the one who lives as love in our home. And it seems to be contagious. I hated, and my children hated. I love now, and now my children love. And it's effortless. That is why I say, with all assurance, "If you live it, we will follow." But you have to live it, because it is what you expect us to do. Don't expect your family to do anything that you can't do. When you learn it, then you can go teach it.

When you start to really live The Work, your family will follow, there's nothing you can do to stop them, because they are all living the way you have been teaching anyway, and they will continue to follow your teachings—not by what you say, but by the way you live. In the peace of that, they'll follow you. It may take a while, because they may not trust you or believe you, they may just believe that you are in another tricky maneuver again. But, if you live this Work, there's no trick to it, it's the real thing, it's love. And eventually they come to trust that love. I can say anything to my children, and it's always my truth. And

they know not to ask me if they don't want
the truth. I am someone to trust.

If I see a mother hitting her child on the
street, I might go up and say, "Sweetheart, I
know how painful it is to hit my own child, I
have done that too. I've been there. How can I
help?" Love doesn't stand by—it moves with
even greater speed, greater clarity. It includes
the mother and the child. To help the mother
is to help the child. And inside me I know
that I'm not doing it for either of them, but
for myself, for my own sense of what is right

for me. So activism becomes very personal, and in my experience more effective as well as kinder.

When we investigate, eventually the dam breaks, and we are just arms open. One way to do this is to take your Worksheet and read the turnarounds to your mother. "Mom, I have been looking at you all my life, and today I began to look at me, and here is what I found: that I manipulate you, that I don't respect you, and that I am learning how to, so please be patient with me, I'm really trying."

It's a whole new field, there is nothing like presence, it's very exciting. And the way you treat your mother is the way you'll treat your husband and your children, because we're not dealing with people here; we're dealing with concepts. This living it, rather than talking it or thinking it, but living it, the living truth—it's a very good place to be.

One day, a few years after I first found The Work inside me, my sons began to fight in our living room. I was sitting on the couch, right next to them. They were two grown men, in their twenties, and here they were on the floor, wrestling and pummeling each other, and both yelling, "Mom, Mom, make him stop!" All I saw were two men trying to connect, not knowing another way. I sat there just watching them, just loving them, and in that moment I didn't have the slightest thought of intervening. There was no doing, there was no trickery to it. And suddenly they noticed, and they stopped fighting. I loved that they found their own solution. And that was the last time they ever fought.

Your children are just there to give you your freedom; they are God disguised as your children, giving you everything you need. You have a great thing to work with. You have what I had to work with, my ex-husband, my mother, my children—and it was all me.

If my child has died, that's the way of it. Any argument with it brings on internal hell. "She died too soon." "I want to see her grow up." "I could have done something to save her." "I was a bad mother." "God is unjust." But her death is reality. No argument in the world can make the slightest dent in what has already happened. Prayer can't change it, begging and pleading can't change it, punishing yourself can't change it, your will has no power at all. You do have the power, though, to question your thought, turn it around, and find three genuine reasons why the death of your child is equal to her not dying, or even better in the long run, both for her and for you. This takes a radically open mind, and nothing less than an open mind is creative enough to free you from the pain of arguing with what is. An open mind is the only way to peace. And as long as you think that you know what should and shouldn't happen, you're trying

to manipulate God. This is a recipe for
unhappiness.

࿇

We are becoming ourselves. We love our
children, there's nothing we can do about that,
we may as well succumb. And in that, they
come to realize that they love us, and there's
nothing they can do about it, and they may as
well succumb. I love that my grown children
will still come into my arms, and that didn't
happen until after 1986, it hadn't happened
since they were young. Today it's the norm
for them to come into my arms, we forget the

age thing, we are just going for something else, the truth. It is nice to sit across from my children, with no words, and be closer than close, closer than can be described.

We have never met our husbands, wives, mothers, fathers, children. Until we investigate our stories about them, we don't have a clue who they are. We're the last to know.

If you think we should be there for you, *you* be there for you! That's not our job. Our name is God, we don't move. We don't move; we are never going to be there for you until you learn to inquire and turn it around. And that's not going to change. You can marry a saint, and it's still not going to change: you won't even perceive that you're living with one. If you think that it was your parents who were out there, you are deceived; there was only God out there, disguised as your parents, giving you what you need. Every time you think your parents should be there for you, don't you experience pain? You miss the reality of it: they're not! When you think you know

what's best for you, it hurts. When you think
they should be here when they're over there,
you hurt, because the reality of it is that they
should be where they are. You're trying to
arrange the chessboard, and it has already
been done! Checkmate!

There is only one way to handle God
disguised as Mother: with unconditional
love. Until you can see your mother as totally
precious all the time, your Work is not done.
That is the beautiful thing about mothers:

just in case you think you have it handled, we
know what button to push.

I lost my children twenty years ago. I came
to see that they were never mine to begin
with. That was an extreme loss: they truly
died to me. And my experience of them now
is intimacy. What their experience of me
is—that's none of my business. Do I want to
be part of their experience? No, I would rather
have my own! How do I share my life? I don't.
I invite them, they say yes or no. They invite
me, I say yes or no.

Ultimately you lose everything. Everything that is thought to be external dies. Everything. You can't have anything. You can't have a husband—it's not a material husband. You can't have children—it's not material children. You can't have one concept. People think that non-attachment has to do with detaching from husband or children or house or car, but it's much more than that. It's a death.

My children pick up their socks now and I don't even ask them to. They understand

now, they love me without condition, and
I had nothing to do with it. Everything I
undo they have to follow, because they are
me. The apparent world is like an echo. The
echo went out from me for forty-three years,
and now it's coming back to me. It's all like
a breath. Like a pebble in the water, all of
the ripples going out all those years and now
they're coming back. I undid the turmoil
and since my children experience me, they're
losing it also. They're losing their attachment
to everything too. They're becoming quiet.
And that's what The Work does for everyone.
That's what I mean by coming back into

itself. They cannot be turbulent if I am not turbulent.

I'm someone to be trusted—without conditions. Even though my children may project it at times, there are no conditions. If they hate me, good. If they love me, good. I'm their story. Without their story, I don't exist.

We don't know how to change; we don't know how to forgive or how to be honest.

We're waiting for an example. You're the one. You are your only hope, because we're not changing until you do. Our job is to keep coming at you, as hard as we can, with everything that angers, upsets, or repulses you, until you understand. We love you that much, whether we're aware of it or not. This whole world is about you. So, to put The Work into action, begin with the voice inside you that's telling you what we should do. Realize that it's actually telling *you* what to do. When it says, "He should pick up the socks," listen to the turnaround "I should pick up the socks," and just do it. Stay in the flow that's effortless and unending. Pick them up until you love it, because it's your truth. And know that the only important house to clean is your mind.

At some point, you may want to go to the deepest pain inside you and clear it up. Do The Work until you see your part in it. And then go to the people you've judged, and apologize; tell them what you've seen about yourself and how you're working on it now. It's all up to you. Speaking these truths is what sets you free.